MACHINES ★ AT WORK

RESCUE HELICOPTERS

BY CYNTHIA ROBERTS

THE CHILD'S WORLD® • MANKATO, MINNESOTA

The Child's World

Published in the United States of America by The Child's World®
1980 Lookout Drive • Mankato, MN 56003-1705
800-599-READ • www.childsworld.com

PHOTO CREDITS

© David M. Budd Photography: cover, 24,, 7 (both) 8, 11, 15, 19
© iStockphoto.com/Eliza Snow: 16
© iStockphoto.com/Jozsef Szasz-Fabian: 3
© iStockphoto.com/sierrarat: 20
© Robert Dyer/Telegram Tribune/Corbis Sygma: 12

ACKNOWLEDGMENTS

The Child's World®: Mary Berendes, Publishing Director;
Katherine Stevenson, Editor

The Design Lab: Kathleen Petelinsek, Design and Page Production

LIBRARY OF CONGRESS CATALOGING-IN-PUBLICATION DATA

Roberts, Cynthia, 1960–
  Rescue helicopters / by Cynthia Roberts.
    p. cm. — (Machines at work)
  Includes bibliographical references and index.
  ISBN 1-59296-835-X (library bound : alk. paper)
  1. Helicopters in search and rescue operations—Juvenile literature.
  2. Emergency vehicles—Juvenile literature. I. Title. II. Series.
  TL553.8.R63 2006
  629.133'352—dc22   2006023296

⭐ Contents

This rescue helicopter is flying over a Colorado city.

⭐ What are rescue helicopters?

Rescue helicopters are special kinds of helicopters. They carry people who are sick or hurt. They rescue people who are in danger. They save people's lives.

⭐ How do rescue helicopters work?

All helicopters have an **engine**. The engine turns large **rotors**. The spinning rotors lift the helicopter off the ground. They let it fly through the air. The **pilot** uses **controls** to fly the helicopter.

rotors

controls

One of these helicopters is carrying someone who is ill. The other one is waiting for the next call.

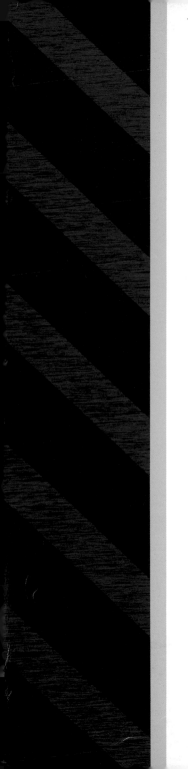

★ Helicopters can do things other airplanes cannot do. Most airplanes can only move forward. Helicopters can fly forward or backward. They can fly up or down. They can turn around or stay still. Flying a helicopter is tricky!

⊛ How are rescue helicopters used?

Some rescue helicopters are used as flying **ambulances**. They take sick or hurt people to **hospitals**. They can go faster than cars or trucks. They can get to places where cars and trucks cannot go.

10

This helicopter is taking off to rescue a sick person. The rotors spin fast to lift it off the ground.

These rescuers are working to free a police car. It had been buried by fast-moving water. ⊛

Some helicopters are used for search-and-rescue work. These helicopters find and save people who are in danger. They save people from forest fires, floods, or sinking ships.

13

★ What is inside a rescue helicopter?

Rescue helicopters carry lots of gear and supplies for helping people. They have at least one **stretcher** for holding a **patient**. They have supplies for taking care of people who are ill or hurt.

14

stretcher

A rescue helicopter's doors can open wide for the stretcher.

cable

This rescuer is being lowered on a cable. The winch lowers him slowly. Other workers make sure the cable doesn't swing too much.

Some rescue helicopters have a winch for rescuing people. The **winch** has a long cable. The cable has a basket or a sling at the end. Sometimes it has a stretcher. The winch winds the cable to lift the person up.

⭐ Who works on a rescue helicopter?

Sometimes another person helps the pilot fly the helicopter. At least one person is there to care for the patient. People who work on rescue helicopters are specially trained. They can help patients before they get to the hospital.

This pilot and worker are talking about their next trip.

This rescue helicopter is off to rescue a skier in the mountains.

⭐ Are rescue helicopters important?

Rescue helicopters are used all over the world. They can fly very fast. They can get to places other ambulances cannot reach. They save lives every day. Rescue helicopters are very important!

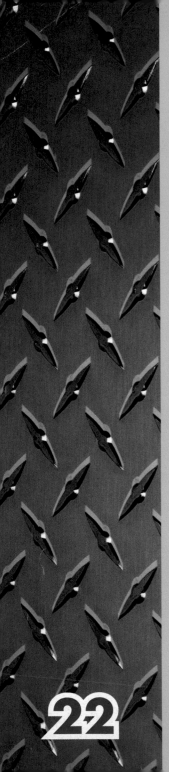

⭐ Glossary

ambulances (AM-byuh-lun-suz) Ambulances are trucks, vans, helicopters, or planes that carry sick or hurt people.

controls (kun-TROHLZ) Controls are parts that people use to run a machine.

engine (EN-jun) An engine is a machine that makes something move.

hospitals (HOSS-pih-tulz) Hospitals are places that take care of people who are sick or hurt.

patient (PAY-shunt) A patient is someone who is getting help for a health problem.

pilot (PY-lut) A pilot is a person who flies an airplane or drives a boat.

rescue (RESS-kyoo) To rescue people is to save them from danger.

rotors (ROH-turz) Rotors are long parts on a helicopter that spin fast and lift the helicopter up.

stretcher (STREH-chur) A stretcher is a bed used to carry people who are ill or hurt.

winch (WINCH) A winch is a machine that raises or pulls things by winding a cable.

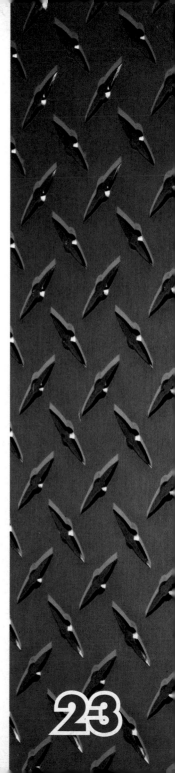

 # Books

Auerbach, Annie, Jesus Redondo (illustrator), and Ican & Moxo (illustrators). *Hero Copter.* New York: Little Simon, 2004.

Beck, Paul. *Flight Test Lab: Helicopters.* San Diego: Silver Dolphin, 2003.

Holden, Henry M. *Rescue Helicopters and Aircraft.* Berkeley Heights, NJ: Enslow Publishers, 2002.

 # Web Sites

Visit our Web site for lots of links about rescue helicopters:
http://www.childsworld.com/links
Note to parents, teachers, and librarians: We routinely check our Web links to make sure they're safe, active sites—so encourage your readers to check them out!

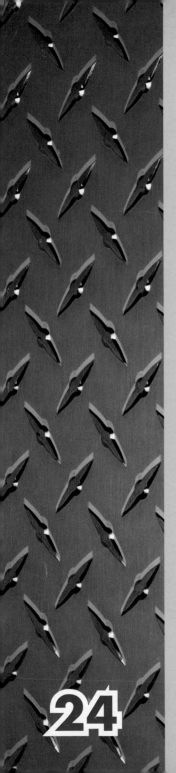

⭐ Index

⭐ About the Author

Even as a child, Cynthia Roberts knew she wanted to be a writer. She is always working to involve kids in reading and writing, and she loves spending time in the children's section of the library or bookstore. Cynthia enjoys gardening, traveling, and having fun with friends and family.